The Fiddler's Tune-Book

SLIP JIGS & WALTZES

FIRST PUBLISHED IN ENGLAND BY DAVE MALLINSON PUBLICATIONS 1999

3 East View, Moorside, Cleckheaton, West Yorkshire, England, BD19 6LD
Telephone +44 (0)1274 876388 *facsimile* +44 (0)1274 865208 *e-mail* **mally@mally.com** *web* **http://www.mally.com**
From the above address you may obtain a full catalogue of DMP titles as well as other books in *The Fiddler's Tune-Book* series

ooOoo

First Printed in England 1999 by Watkiss Studios Limited, telephone +44 (0)1767 313858

ISBN 1-899512-51-9

British Library cataloguing in publication data:
A catalogue record for this book is available from the British Library

ooOoo

Edited by Peter Kennedy

Harmony arrangements, data input and manipulation by David J Taylor
Text set in Caslon; music engraved in Petrucci within *Finale*; pages laid out within *QuarkXPress*

ooOoo

The cover and frontispiece drawing of Charles Benfield of Idbury, Oxfordshire was drawn by A Van Anrooy, RI

ooOoo

Introduction

The triple awakening

THIS book comes in response to the re-discovery of the much neglected triple-time jig and waltz rhythms once widely used for all kinds of traditional dancing in Britain and Ireland. Before the end of the nineteenth century this triple rhythm was used for long sets, the *country* or *contra* dances and in the square sets or *quadrilles,* which in waltz rhythm were know as *cotillions.* Both jigs and waltzes were used for these community formation dances, but, of course, the waltz itself swept the fashionable ballrooms as a 'round dance' for individual couples. There were many varieties of couple waltzes, but the most distinctive from the straightforward, old-fashioned waltzes were the *mazurkas*—also known as 'polka mazurkas'—and the *varsoviana,* presumably of Polish origin, which once rivalled the lively duple-time polkas, highlands and schottisches featured in other books in this series.

The decline in jig-hopping

Probably the most obvious reason for the decline in the popularity of the triple-time jigs, also know as *slip jigs* or *hop jigs,* was the decline in the the special rhythmical skill required by both fiddlers and dancers. In England only a few nine-eight time tunes and dances were still current at the start of the 20th century.

Particularly at Christmas time, perhaps partly due to Charles Dickens, children's parties were still enjoying that memorable long dance, now known in the States as the *Virginia Reel,* but in those days danced to and known by the name of *Sir Roger de Coverley* or, perhaps not by the children, as *The Maltman Comes on Monday.* Half a century later, a similar dance in Northumberland, which highlighted the strip the willow figure and was known as *Drops of Brandy,* no longer used the $\frac{9}{8}$ tune but employed a highland schottische version of *Yankee Doodle* and the hop-jig three-step had given way to the step-hop two-step.

The on-going off-beat drive

So what is the skill of the triple rhythm? As I have said in the introductions to the other *Fiddler's Tune-Books* (I hope you read them) the biggest clue lies in paying attention to the off-beats. In this case, of course, we have two off-beats, the *cha*s of the *oom-cha-cha.* I reckon the last 'cha' to be of prime importance, in order to spirit the dancers along. We know how disastrous it can be, in a double jig like *The Irish Washerwoman,* for instance, for the fiddler to dig the main beats themselves. You literally dig the dancers into the ground deeper and deeper and there is therefore no forward drive. The same applies here; if you do the same in a waltz, for example, the monotony of it will not only kill the dancers but probably any other musicians as well.

The secret lies, again I have said this before, in control of speed. Not just practising slowly or fast but being able to slow down or speed up; to do this slowly or fast and, at the same time, employ the ever-changing rhythmical shape similar to that used by a cantering horse. Remember that there are not just two off-beats in a triple jig but three sets of off-beats to use in the way I have previously described.

A collector's collection

You may ask me how I came across all these tunes. The answer is that since 1950 I have been travelling the rural areas recording the more elderly traditional musicians, most of whom, at some time, have played for dancing. On the whole they have learned their tunes by ear from their parents or from local players of the their district. Since that date, younger musicians have not been so community-rooted in their own localities and, in addition, have had the opportunity to listen to radio and records and to learn from players in other areas.

It was because of a need to find standard versions, particularly for country dance bands, that the *Fiddler's Tune-Book* series was born. In addition, like singers using broadsides, I have come across old out-of-print music collections and hand-written manuscripts. From these I have jotted down those versions of tunes, most of which I have heard at some time or other, which I felt might be of value, in the first instance for my own dance band, but now, in retirement, I dedicate them to future generations.

The oral tradition

However, these books should not be used simply to provide new tunes to impress your friends. Traditional music is always played more effectively when it is learned by ear. Whenever possible I would advise fiddlers to learn from live or recorded players. These tune books should help you to extend your repertoire, but as soon as possible you should try and depart from the written page. Have it there to remind but please don't play traditional music only from the written page. The tradition can only be continued if there is a give-and-take between the fiddler and the folk.

PETER KENNEDY, FOLKTRACKS 1998

——— ooOoo ———

The Central Library of Ethnic Folktracks comprises Reference Library, Tape and Film Archive, Folk Shop & Folkatek Studio. Heritage House, 16 Brunswick Square, Gloucester, England, GL1 1UG, telephone +44 (0)1452 415110, facsimile +44 (0)1452 503643, e-mail: peter@folktrax.freeserve.co.uk

The Gloucester Folkatek is situated in a Georgian terrace in a quiet central city square, adjacent to the docks, with convenient parking and it provides valuable resource and study facilities to a broad range of international organisations and interested individuals and to all those concerned with a wide range of traditions in the worlds of education and entertainment.

The Kennedy Collection was built up over four generations of a famous Scottish singing family which included the famous David Kennedy and his daughter, Marjorie Kennedy-Fraser, who collected *The Songs of the Hebrides,* Douglas Kennedy, who carried on the folk music work begun in England by Cecil Sharp and the Karpeles family, who also worked with Sharp. Peter Kennedy, who started recording in Britain and Ireland in 1950, has built up the most extensive international collection of audio and video recordings. These recordings cover local seasonal customs, children's playground games, singers, storytellers, fiddlers, pipers, box-players and other instrumentalists.

The Reference Library houses over 4,000 specialist books as well as manuscripts, photographs, magazines and journals concerned with oral traditions: anthropology and ethno-musicology, gypsies and tinkers, folklore and language, folk life and folk crafts etc. There is also a well-equipped recording and editing studio, audio and video, using both digital and analogue systems. These facilities are open daily to students and researchers by prior appointment.

Folktracks Recordings, available since 1975, provide over 300 CD programmes of authentic field recordings with more items being added to the list every year. Free listings are available or a full catalogue can be purchased.

Published 1998 by Dave Mallinson Publications. Melody arrangements copyright © Folktracks and Soundpost Publications 1998

ANDREW CAREY
(Derby Carey)

ARKLOW LASSES

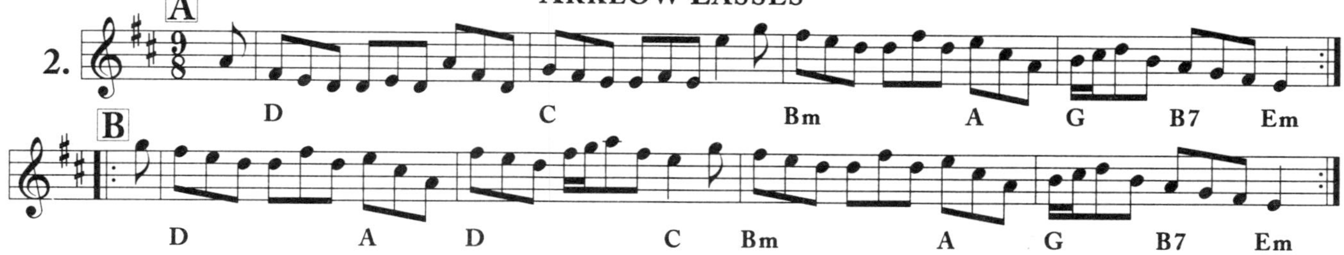

BALTYORAN
(Baltighoran)

THE BANAGHER LASSES

THE BESOM BRUSH

Published 1998 by Dave Mallinson Publications.

Bob and Joan
(Love and Whisky)

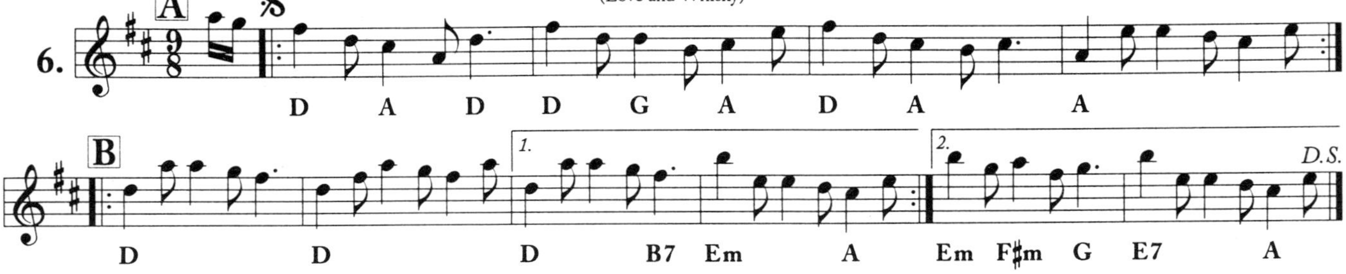

Brose and Butter

Buckskin Breeches

A Bumper at Parting

Camstroden's Rant

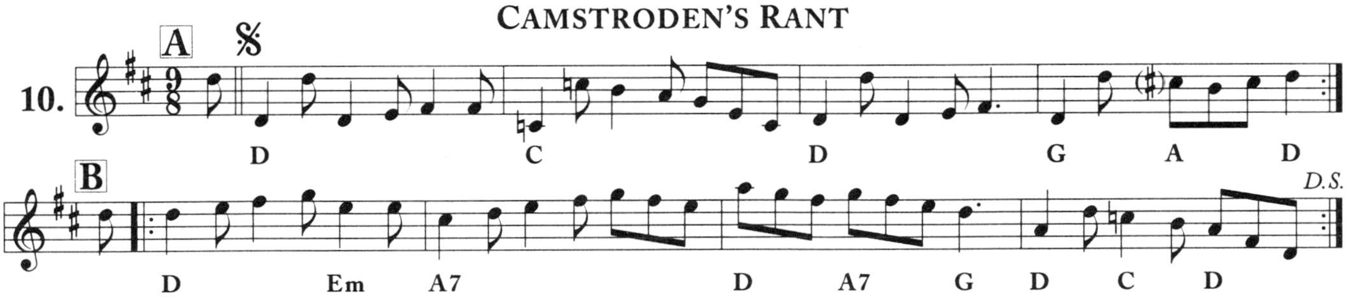

Captain McDonald's Favourite
(The Hawthorn Bush)

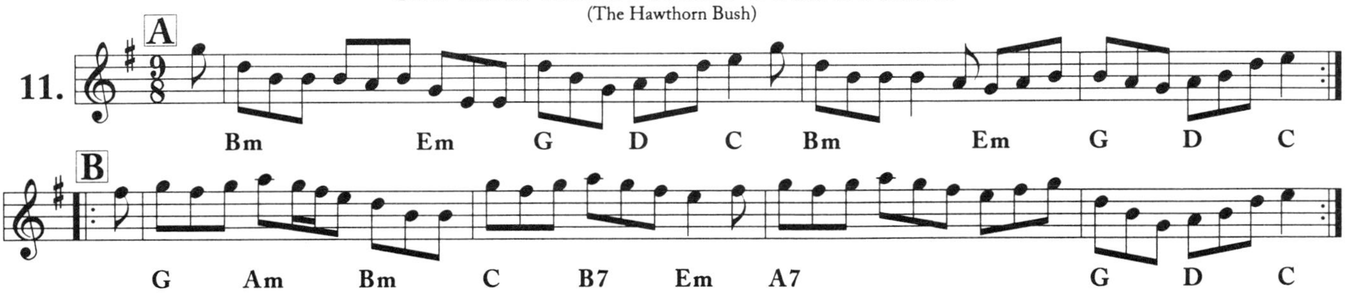

The Cock and the Hen

Curl the Wig

(Leather the Wig; A Whack at the Whigs)

Dress Her Up Fine

(Dress Her Out in Fine Clothes; McCarty's Jig)

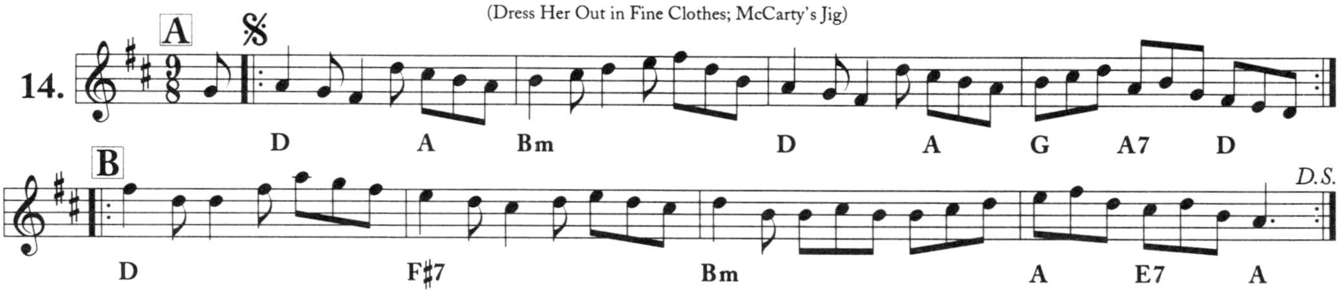

Drive the World Before You

(Waterford Girls)

Drops of Brandy

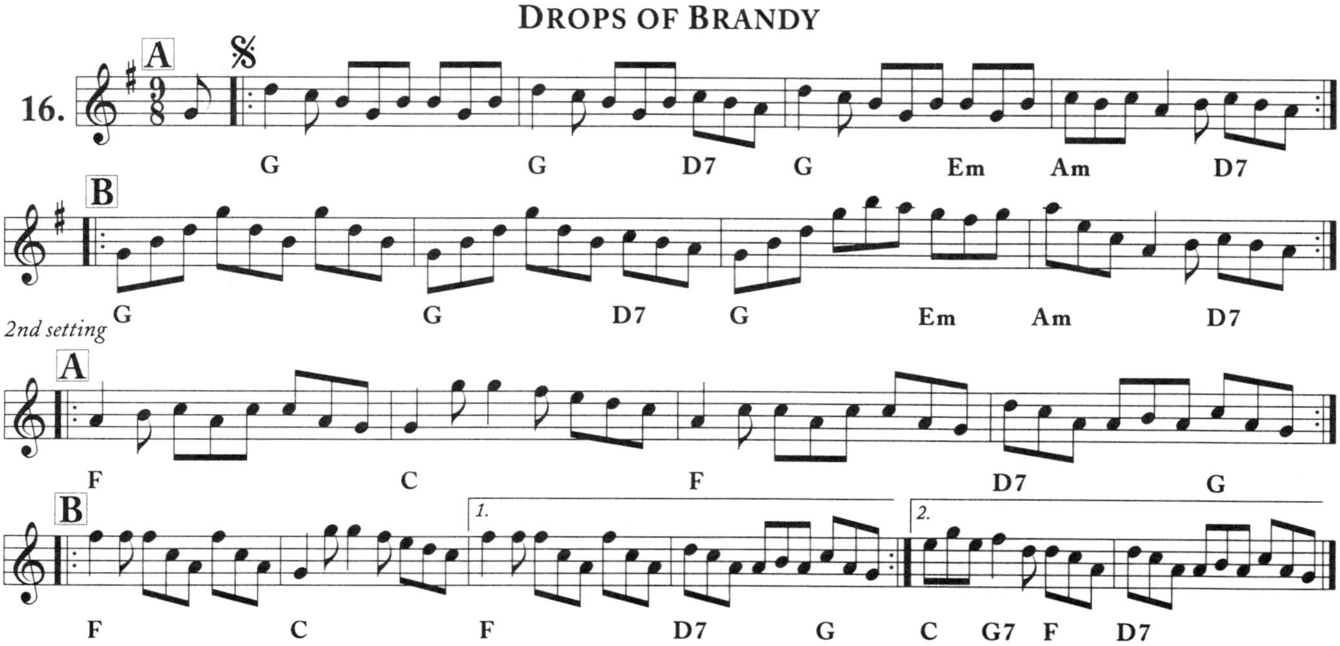

THE DROUGHT
(Drown Drowth)

DRUMMORE LASSES

THE DRUNKEN GAUGER
(The Ganger; The Steampacket)

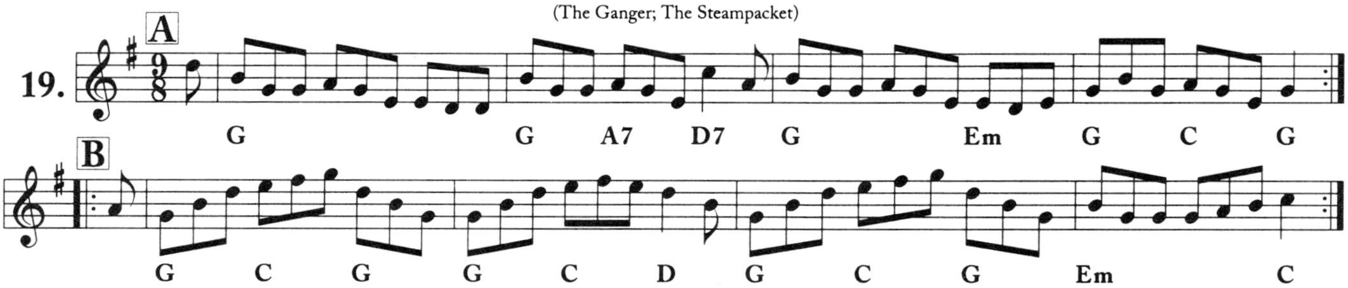

THE DUSTY MILLER
(Top the Candle)

A FIG FOR A KISS
(Two in a Gig)

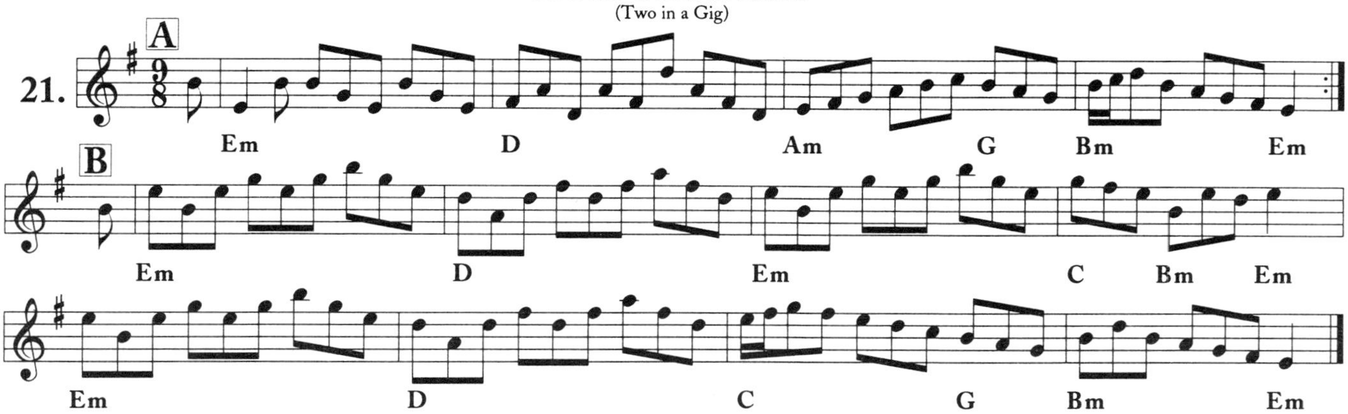

THE FOXHUNTER'S

THE FRESH JUG

GO TO BERWICK, JOCKEY

THE GRINDER

(The Grenadiers; Terry Heigh-ho, the Grinder)

GUSTY'S FROLICS

(Gurty's)

HEY, CA' THRO'

Hey, My Nanny
(Up in the Garret)

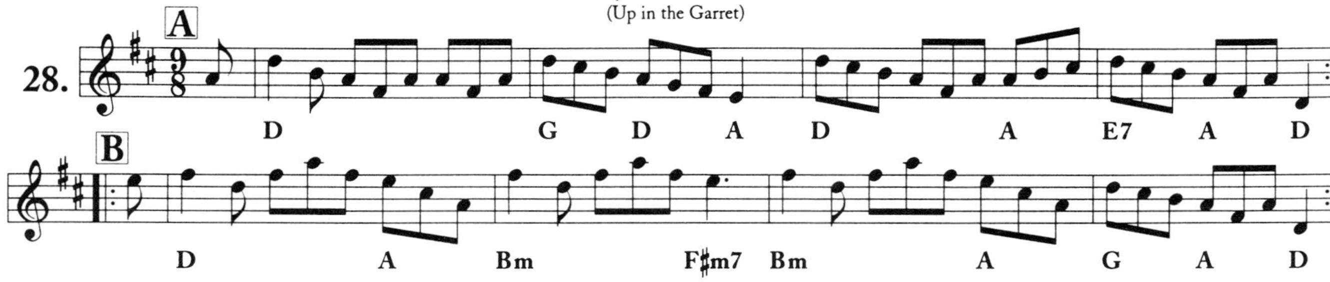

Hills of Tipperary

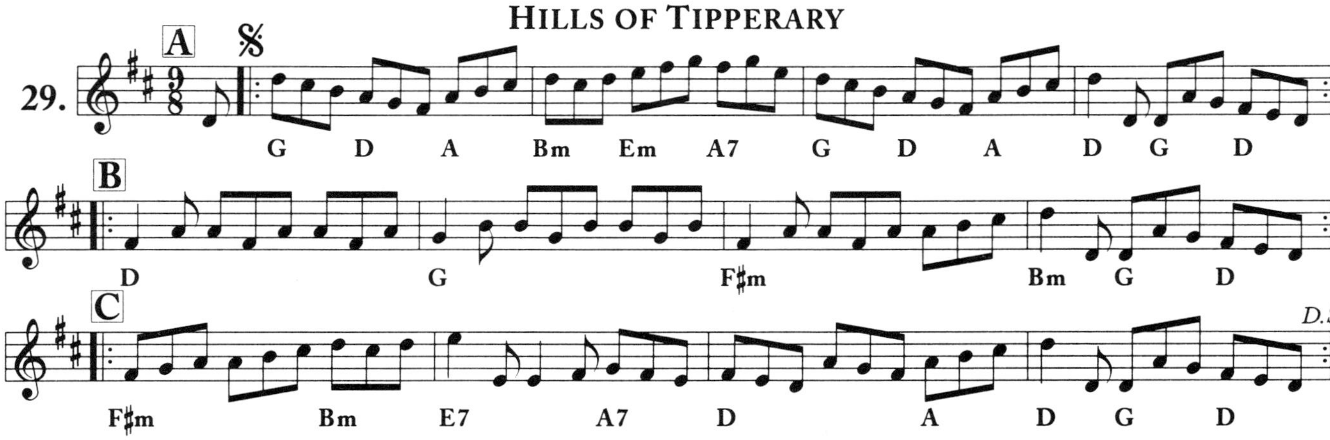

The Hip Doctor

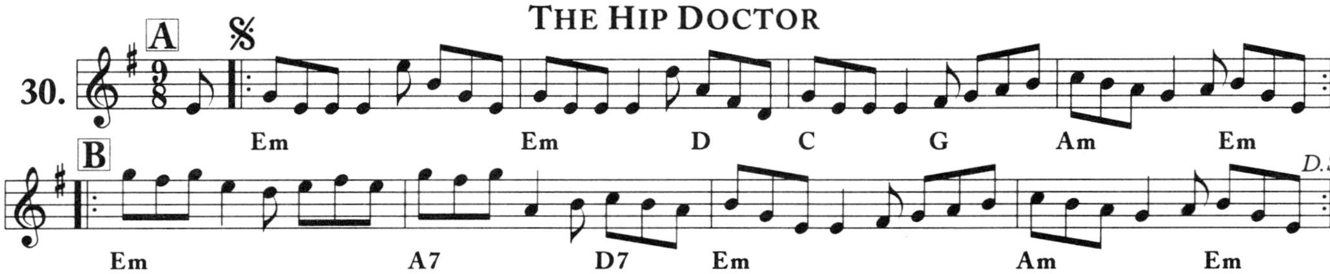

The Humours of Whiskey

The Humours of Woodstown

Hunt the Hare
(The Hibernian Jig)

The Irish Hop Pickers

Jack in the Green

Jack Won't Sell His Fiddle

(I Hae a Wife o' my Ain)

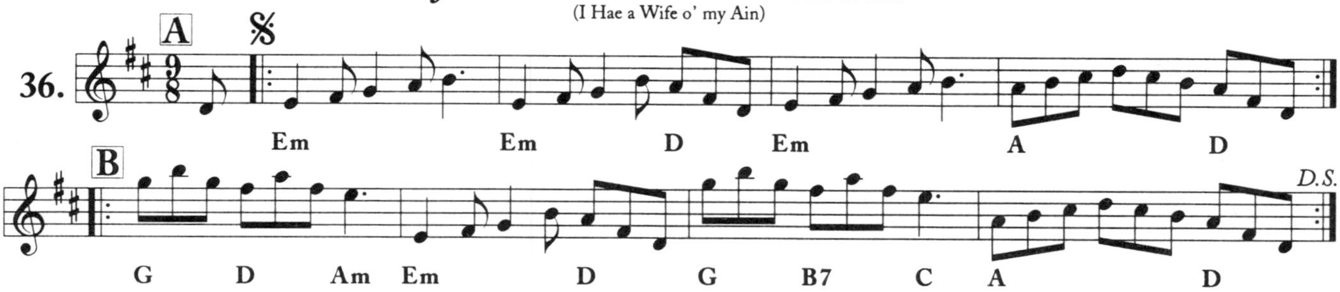

The Kid on the Mountain

Lady Cawdor's

Let Us Awa' to the Wedding

(The Blithesome Bridal; Come fy Let's A' to the Bridal; I'm the Boy for Bewitching Them; The Jolly Pedlars)

The Limerick Jig

Looby Light

Mad Moll

(The Peacock Followed the Hen)

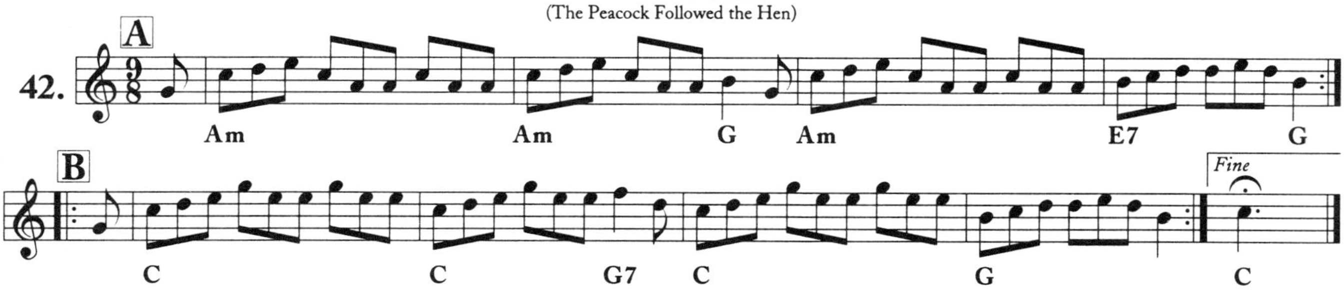

Maggie's Tocher

The Maid's Complaint

Melancholy Martin

The Merry Old Woman

Miss Blewit's Jig

(Barney Brallaghan; The Master Tailor's Lilt)

Miss Brown's Fancy

Miss Butler's Fancy

Moll Roe in the Morning
(Ditherum Doodle; One Bumper at Parting)

50.

Mount the Hair and Curl It
(Comb the Hair and Curl It)

51.

The Night of the Fun
(Dublin Boys; Dublin Streets; Last Night's Fun)

52.
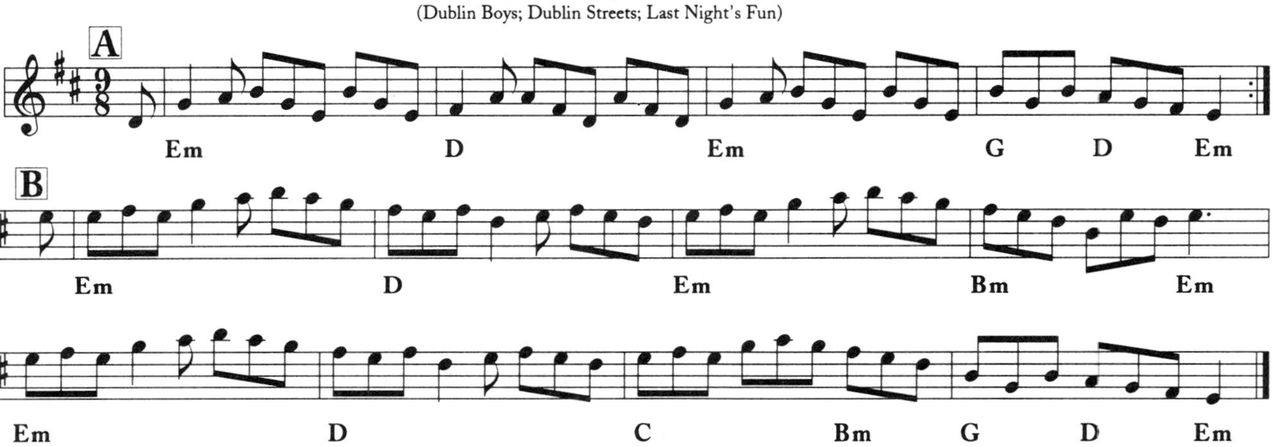

The Old Hag in the Corner

53.

The Old Milk Churn
(A Fig for a Kiss)

54.
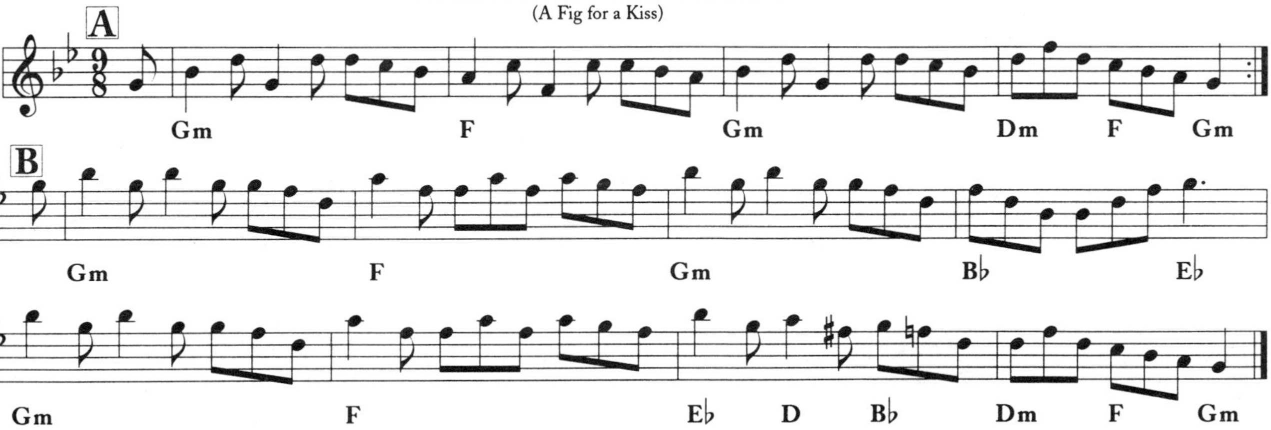

Old Mother Goose

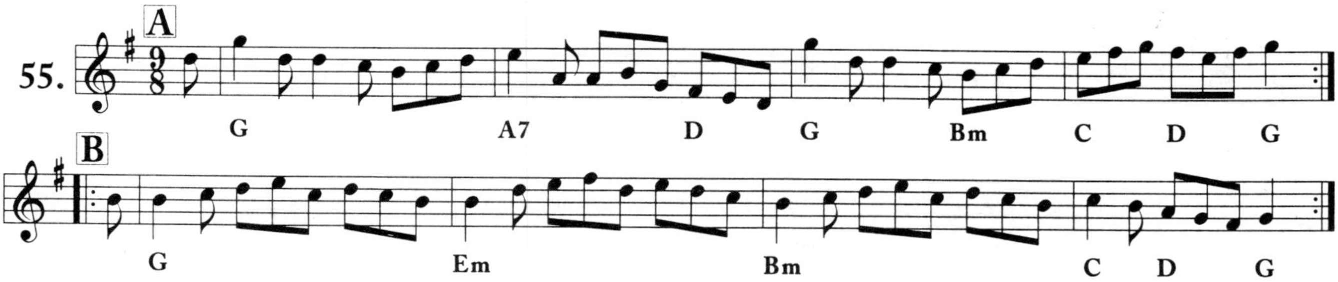

Open the Door for Three

Paddy, Now won't You be Aisy

Paddy O'Snap

(Quick! We Have but a Second!)

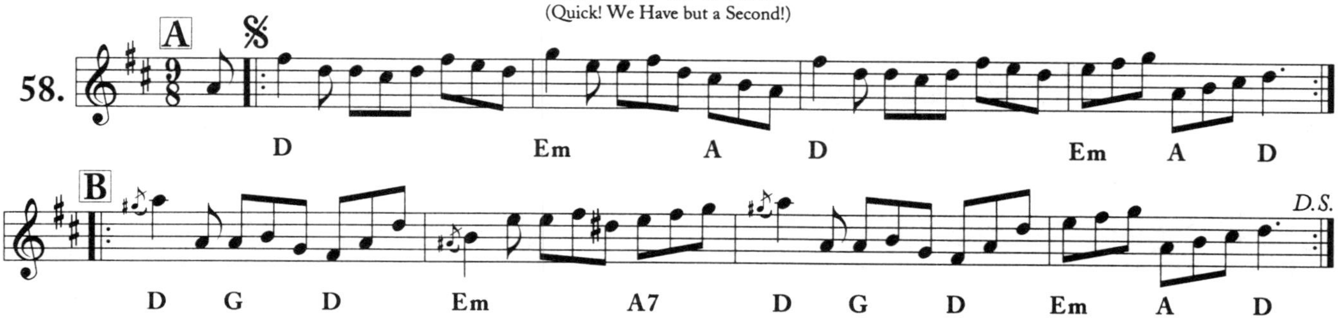

Phillip McHugh

(Sir Philip McHugh)

The Piper's Maggot

Plumkum

(The Munster Gimlet; Will You Come Down to Limerick?)

Polthogue

(The Humours of Ballymanus; Newton Lasses)

The Rakes of Kilkenny

(The Barn Door; The Highway to Kilkenny)

The Rakes of Westmeath

Rattlin' Roarin' Willie

65.

Red Stockings

66.

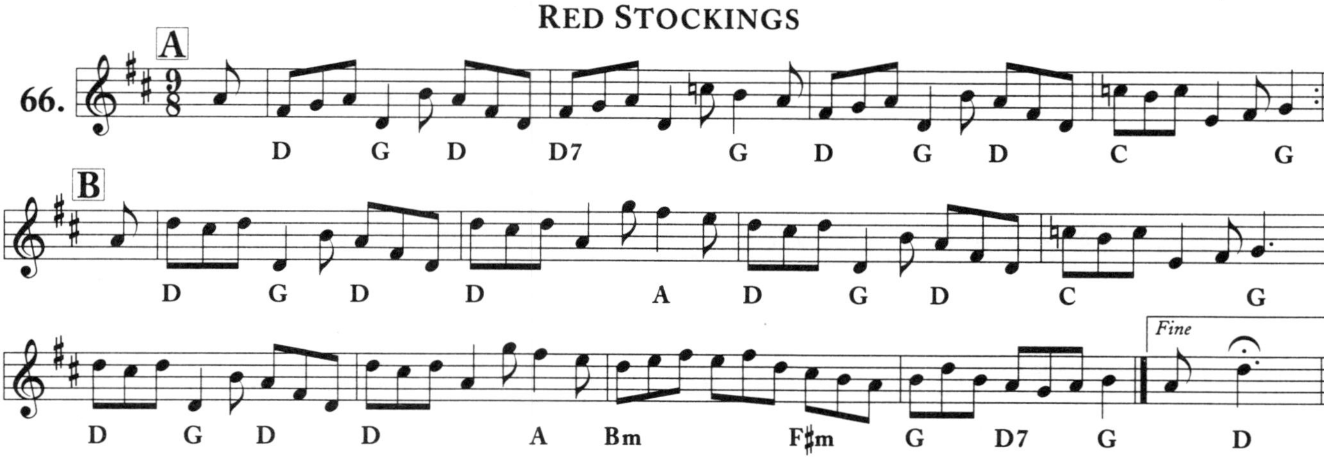

Ride a Mile

Cummilum; I Don't Care)

67.

The Road to Sligo

68.

The Rocky Road to Dublin

69.

Roudlum No. 1

70a.

Roudlum No. 2

70b.

Rouse It

71.

The Shamrock

Sheila's Kiss

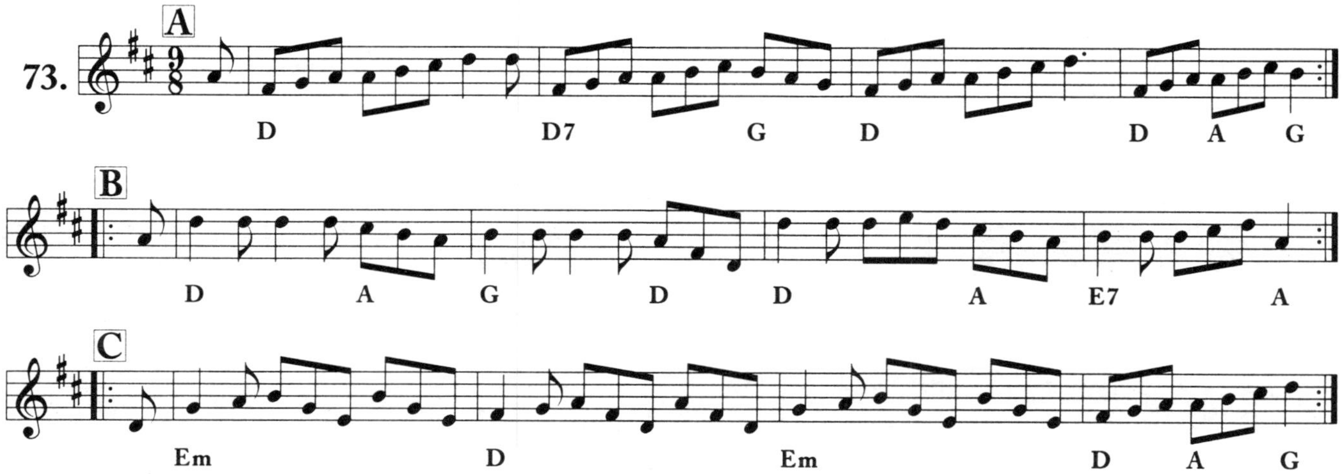

Shuffle and Cut

Sir Harry's Favourite

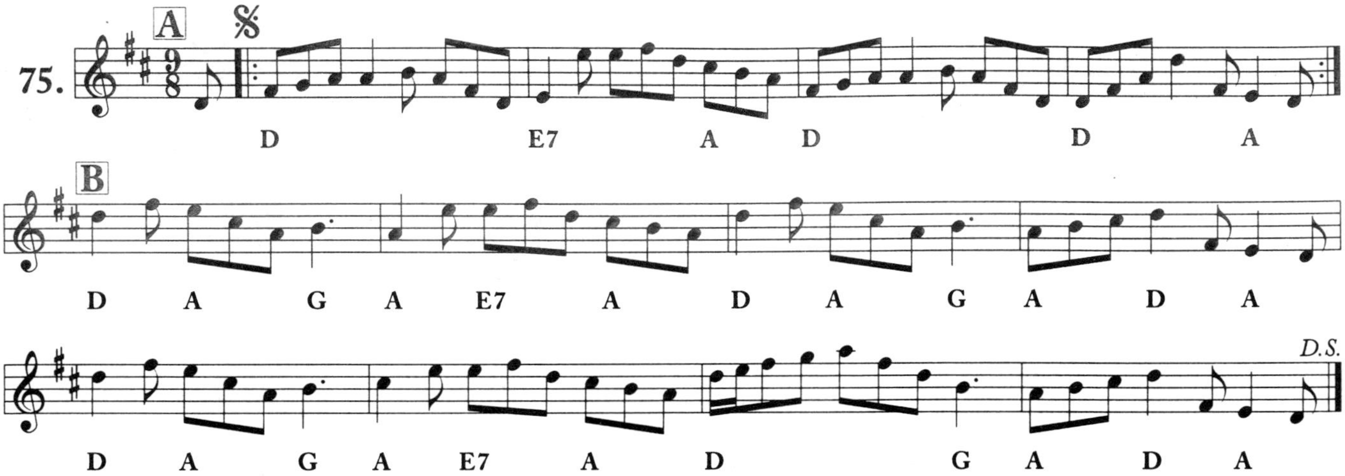

Sir John Scott's Favourite

Sir Roger de Coverley

(The Maltman Comes on Monday)

Spatter the Dew

The Spirit of Whiskey

The Sport of the Chase

The Swaggering Jig

Tea in the Morning

Published 1998 by Dave Mallinson Publications. Melody arrangements copyright © Folktracks and Soundpost Publications 1998

TEAGUE'S RAMBLE

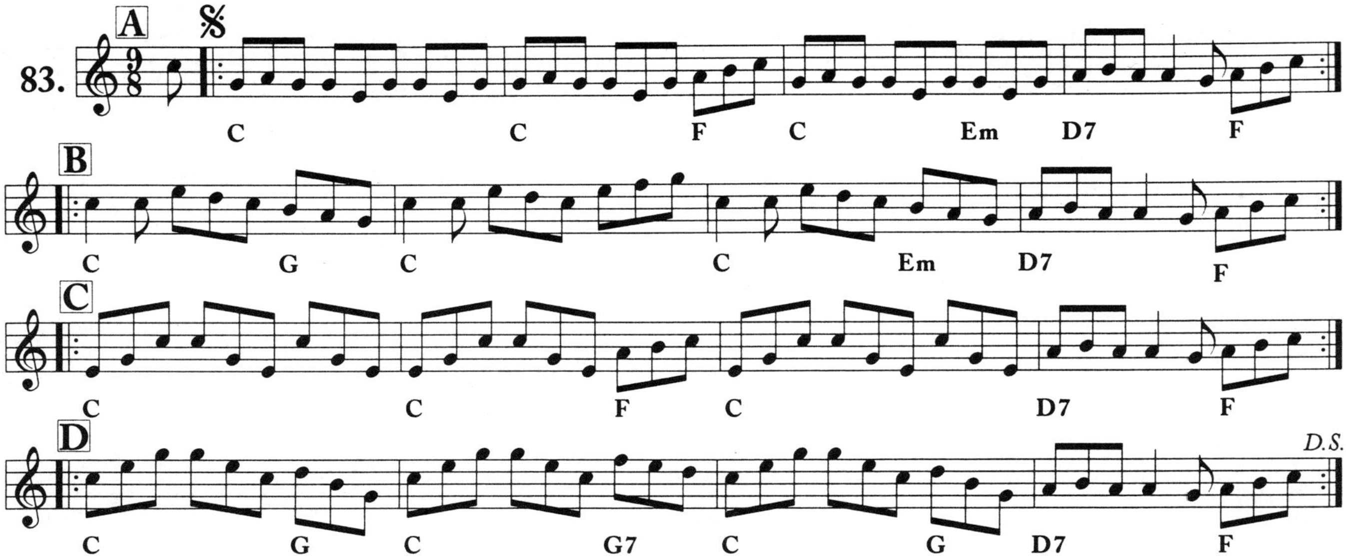

TIGHT BREECHES

(Whisky and Beer)

THE TIME OF DAY

THE TWOPENNY POSTMAN

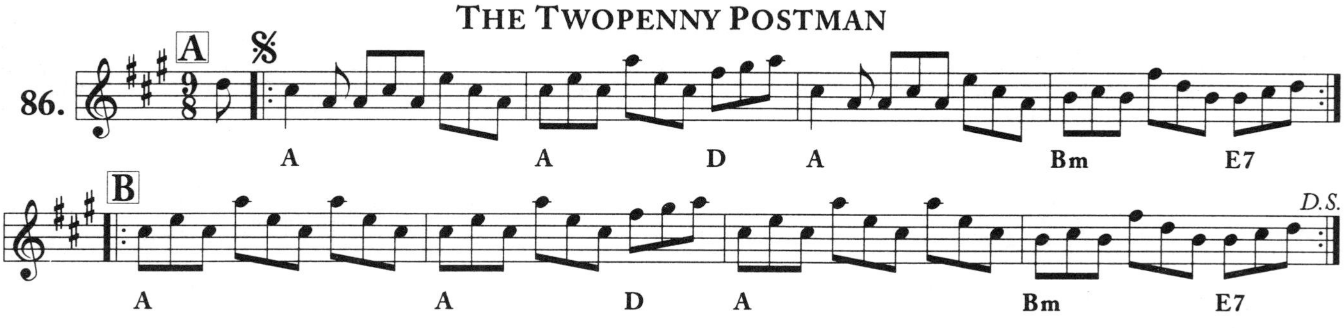

WELLINGTON'S COMING

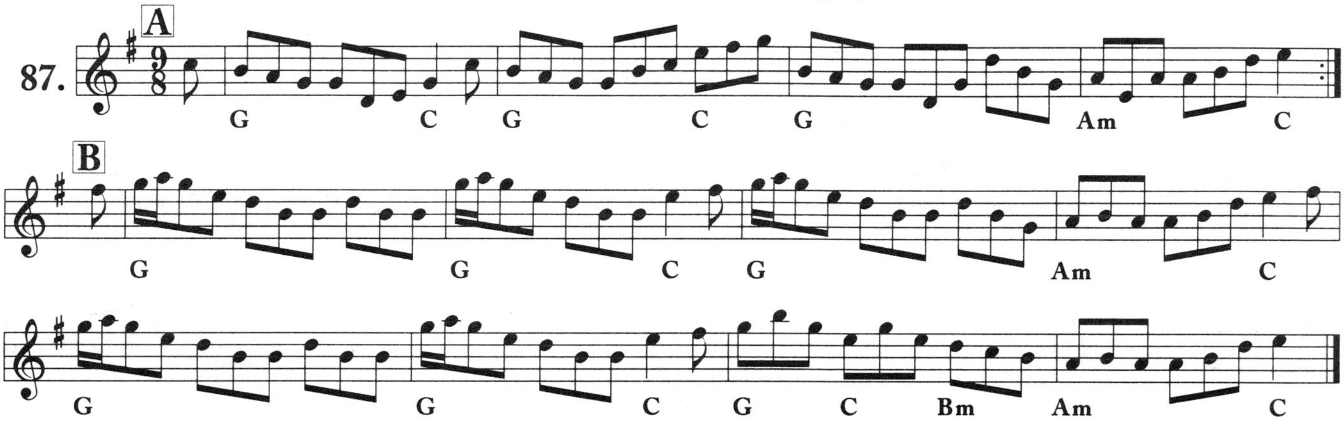

The Wishing Well

The Woods of Fanaid

Yellow Leggings

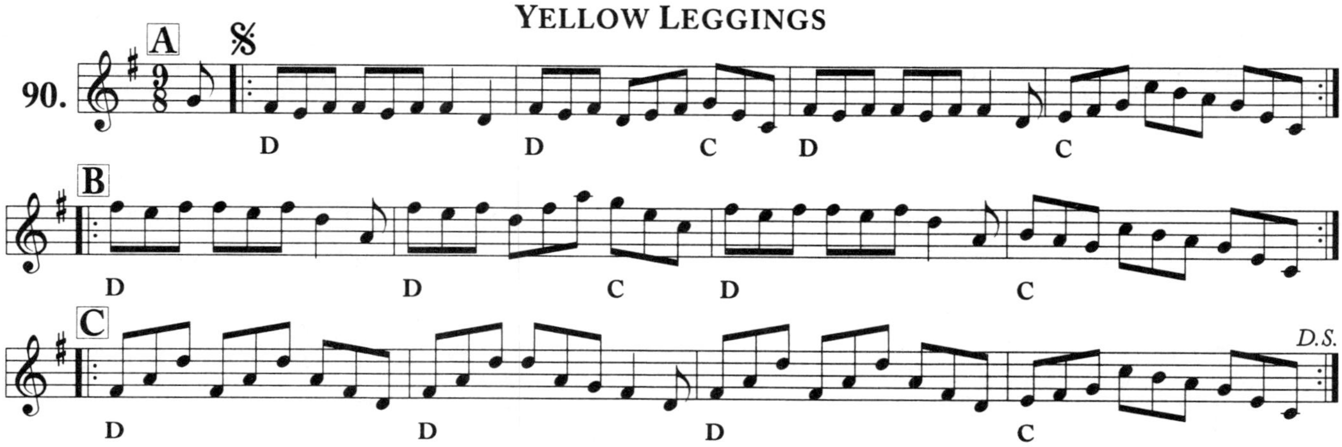

Aaron's

The Absent-Minded

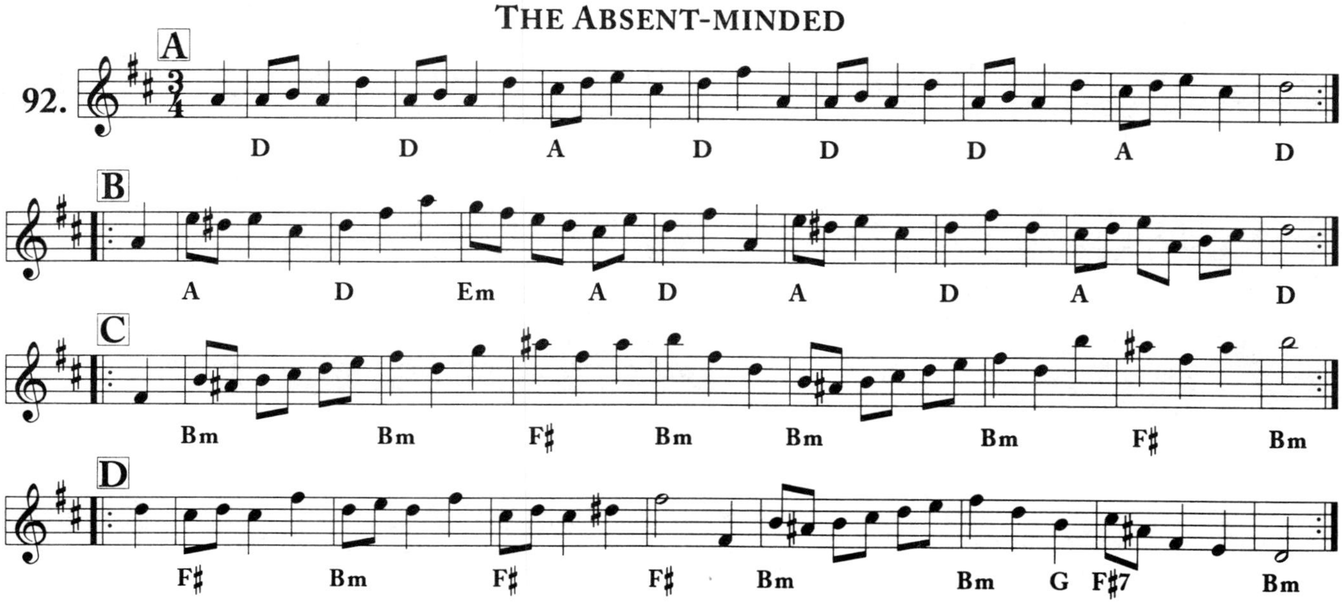

THE ALLENTOWN

93.

Arabella's

The Bandits'

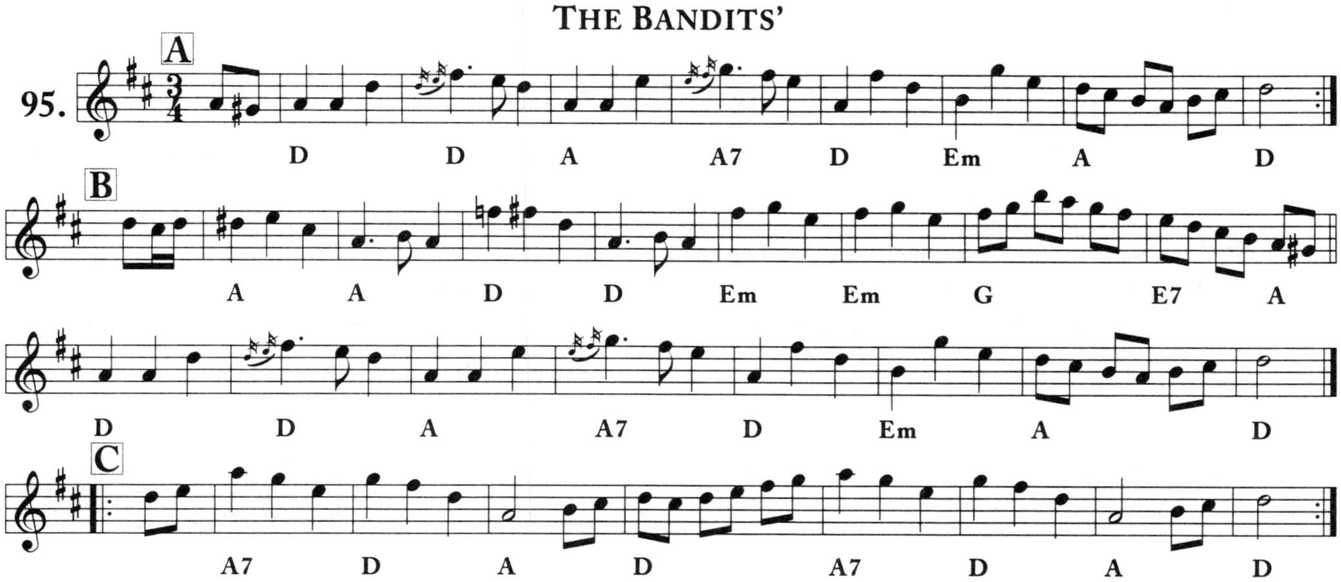

Bartholomew's

The Bath

The Bohemian

The Brunswick

Buckingham's

The Bugle

Buonaparte's

BUY A BROOM

103.

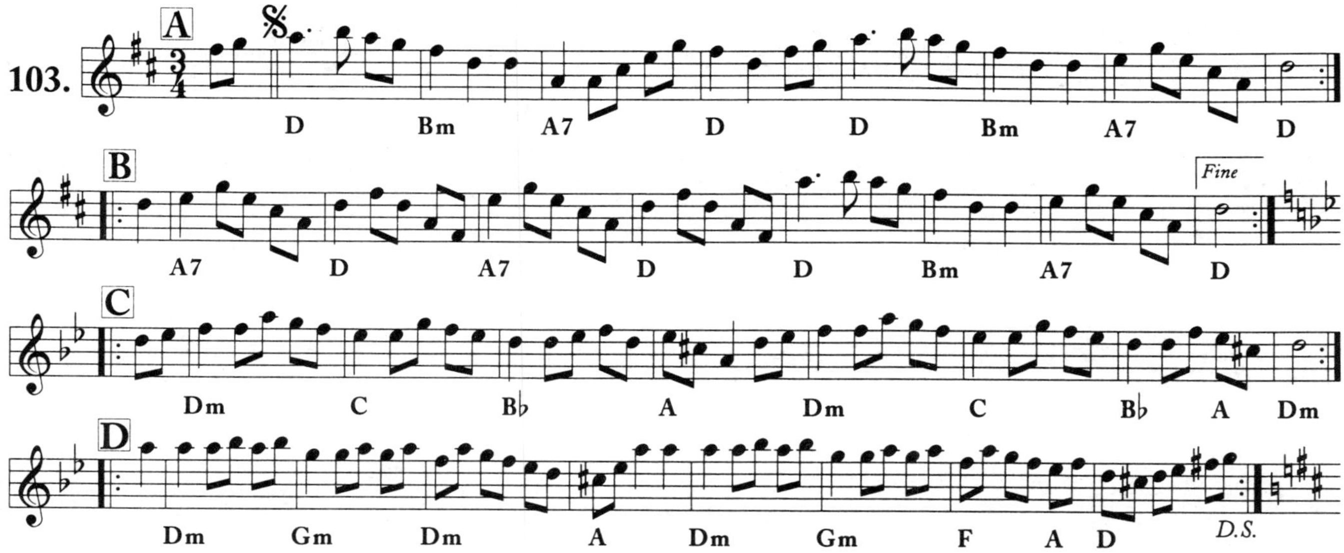

THE CALABRIAN

104.

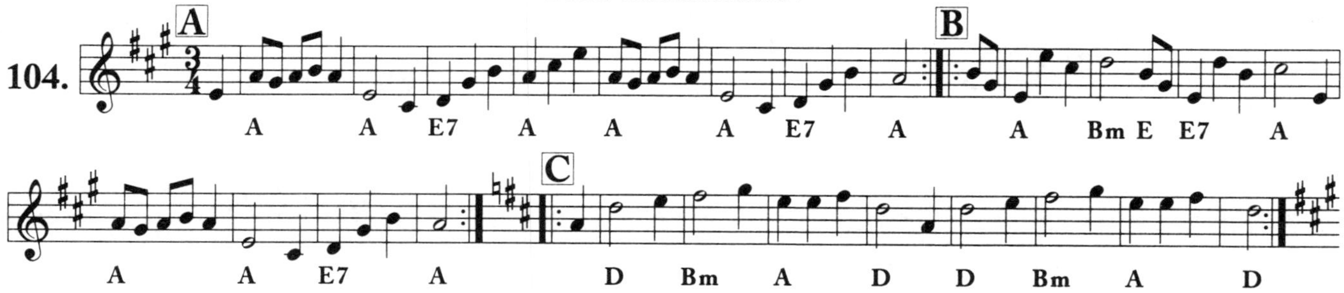

CAPTAIN CUFFE'S

105.

CASEY'S

106.

The Catch-in-time

107.

The Coburg

108.

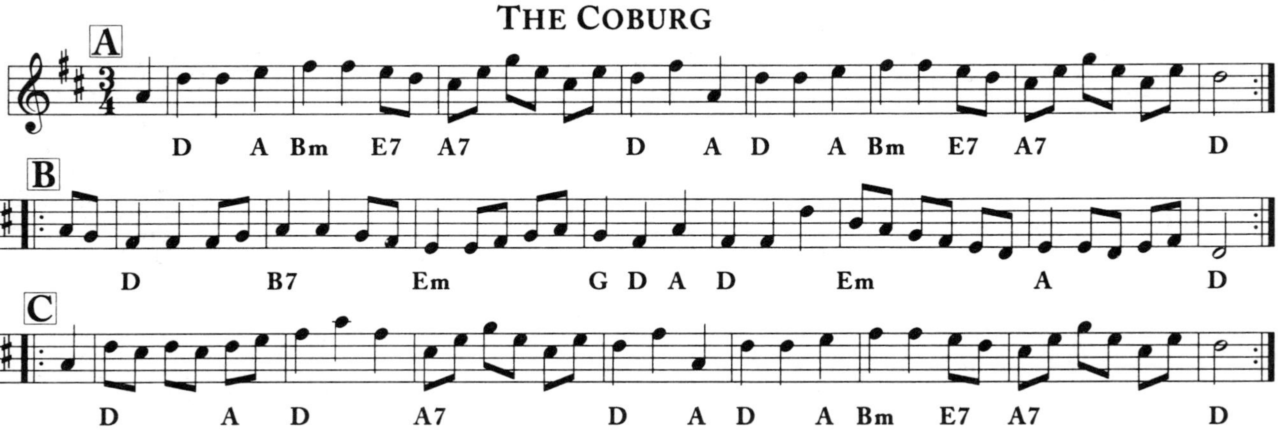

The Comet

109.

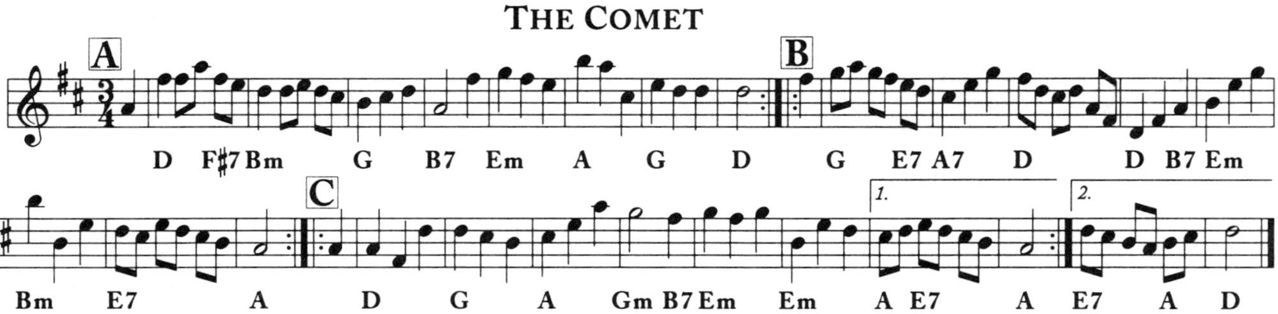

The Copenhagen

110.

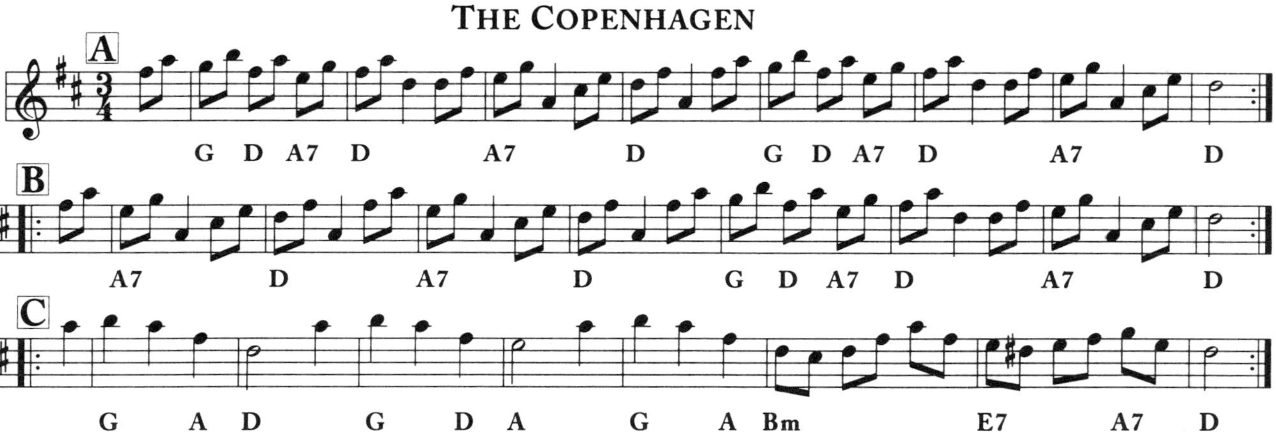

The Cossack

111.

THE DAIRYMAID'S

THE DERRYDOWN

THE DUKE OF BEDFORD'S

THE DUKE OF YORK'S

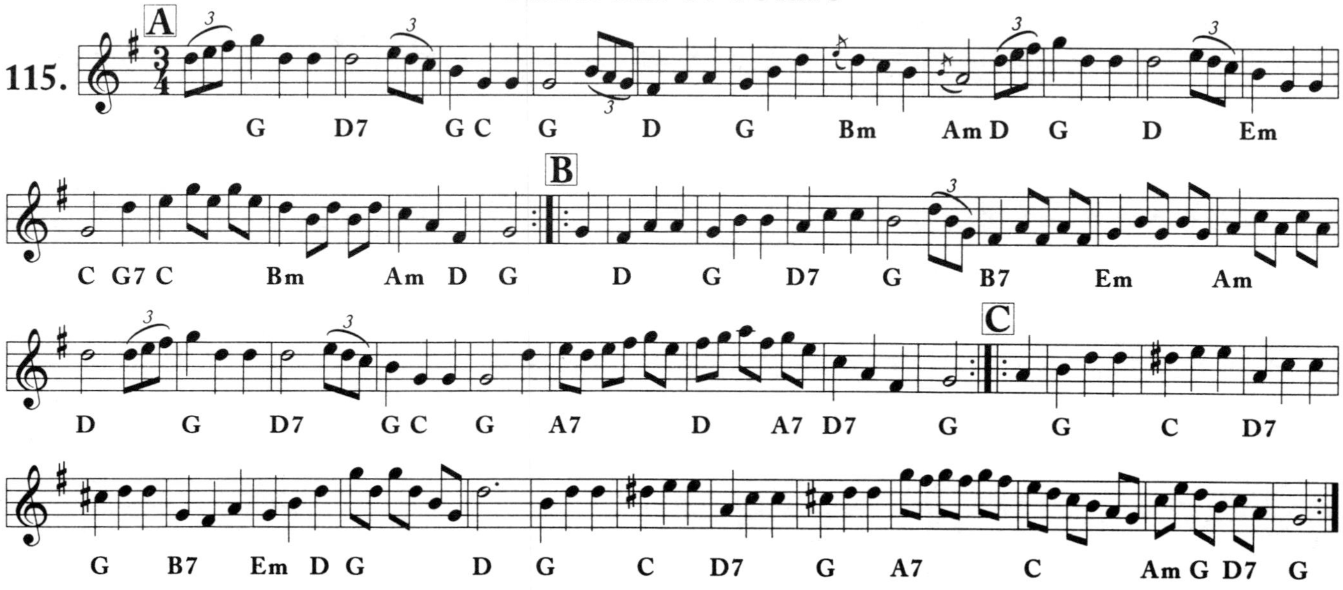

The Easter

Edinburgh Castle

The Evening Star

The Faint-Hearted

The Favourite

Ferrybank

General Graham's

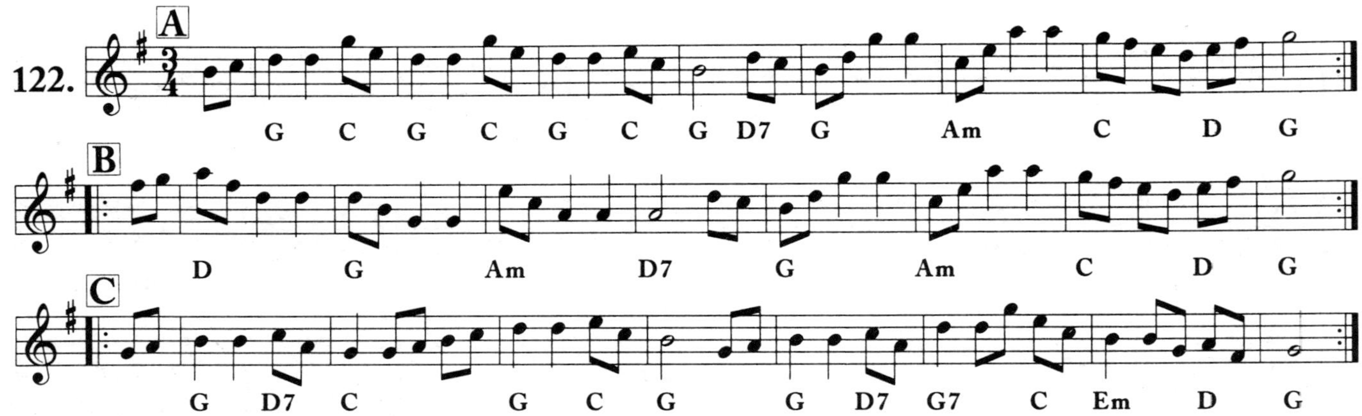

Golden Tresses

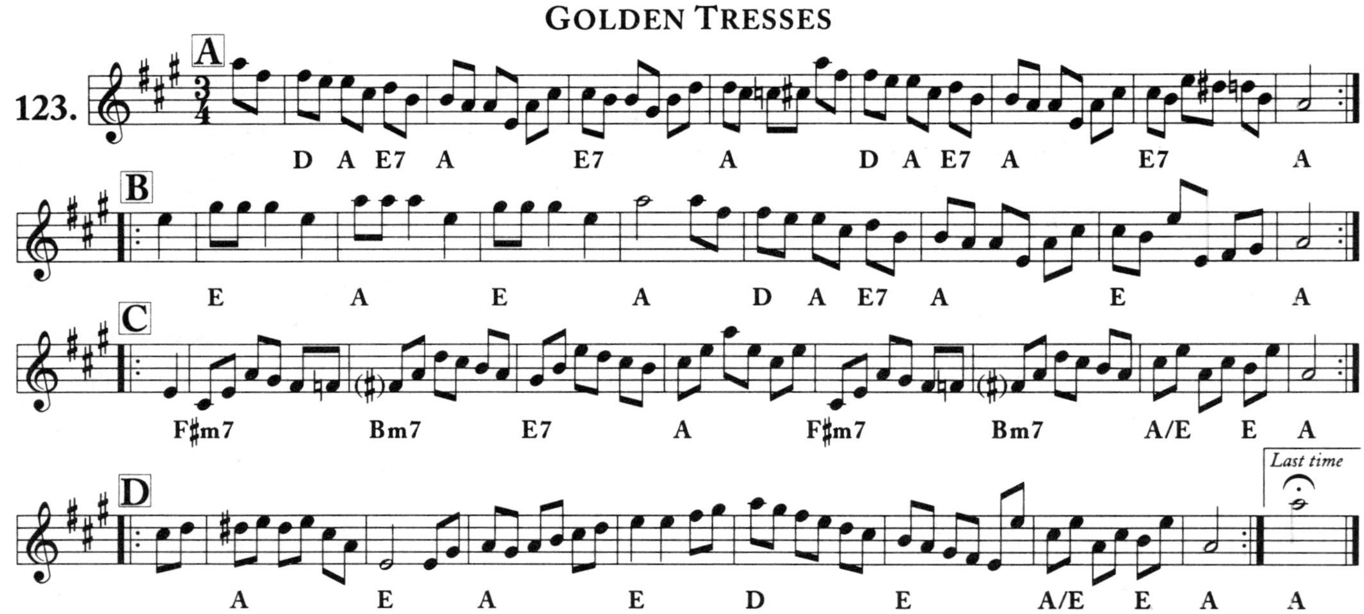

The Grand Central

The Grand Eastern

125.

The Grand Northern

126.

The Grand Southern

127.

THE GRAND WESTERN

128.

GREYSTONES

129.

THE GUARACHA

130.

THE HARVESTERS'

131.
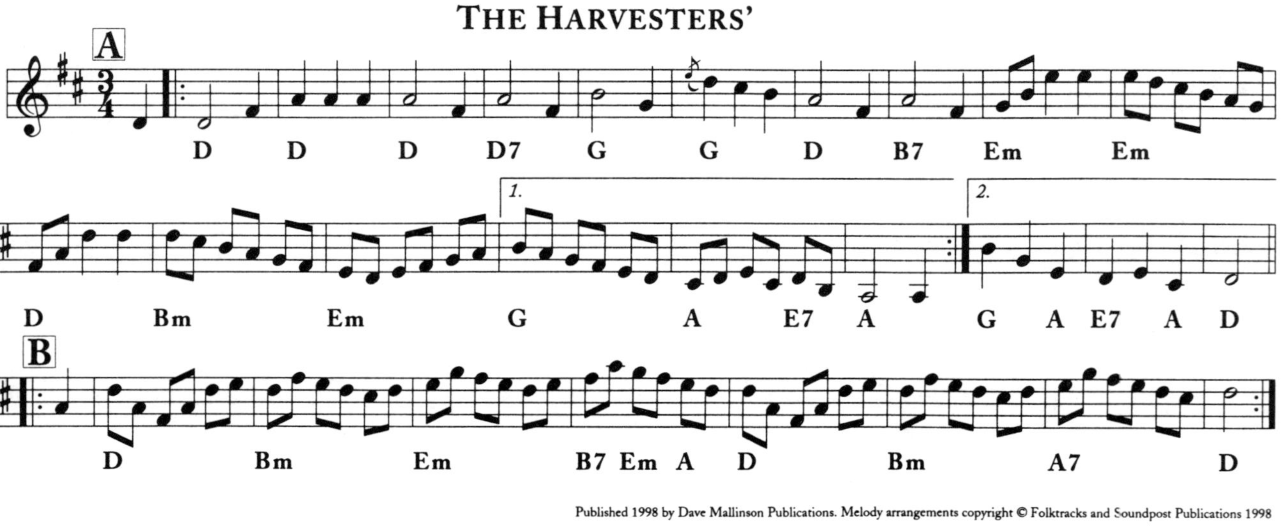

Henry Gardiner's

Hilltop

Indiana

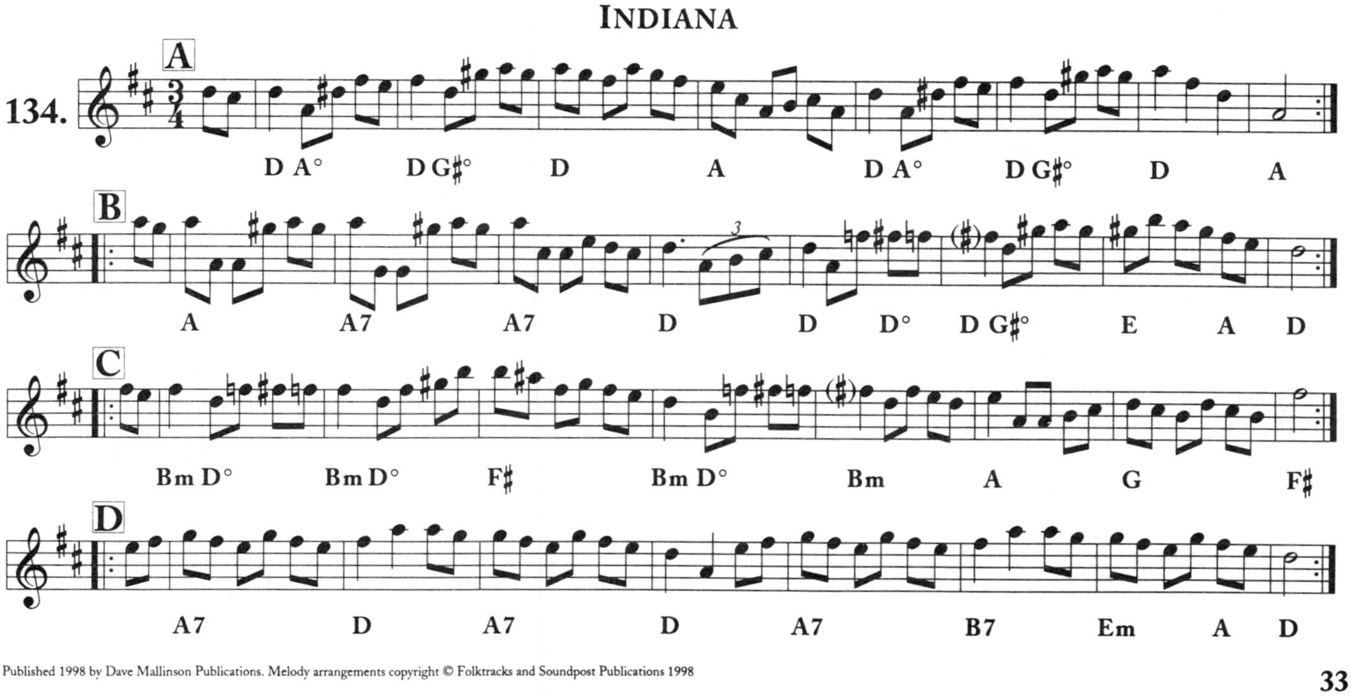

IRISHTOWN

JEAN'S

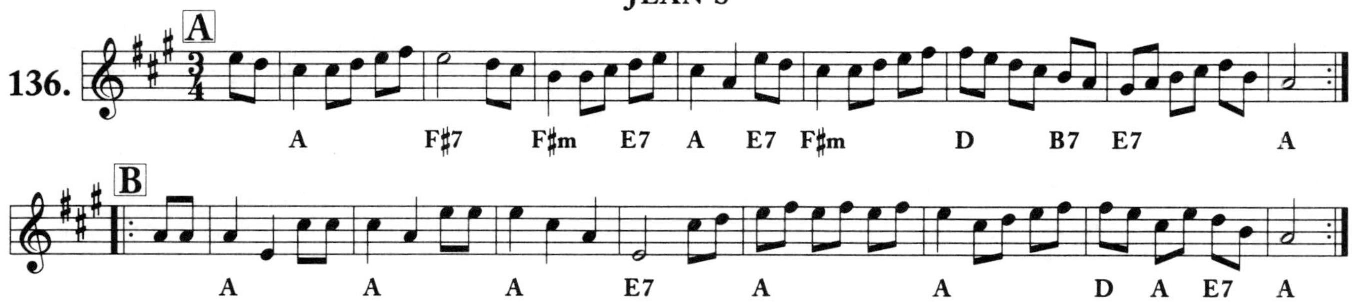

JONESBOROUGH

KATIE'S NEW

KILBERRY

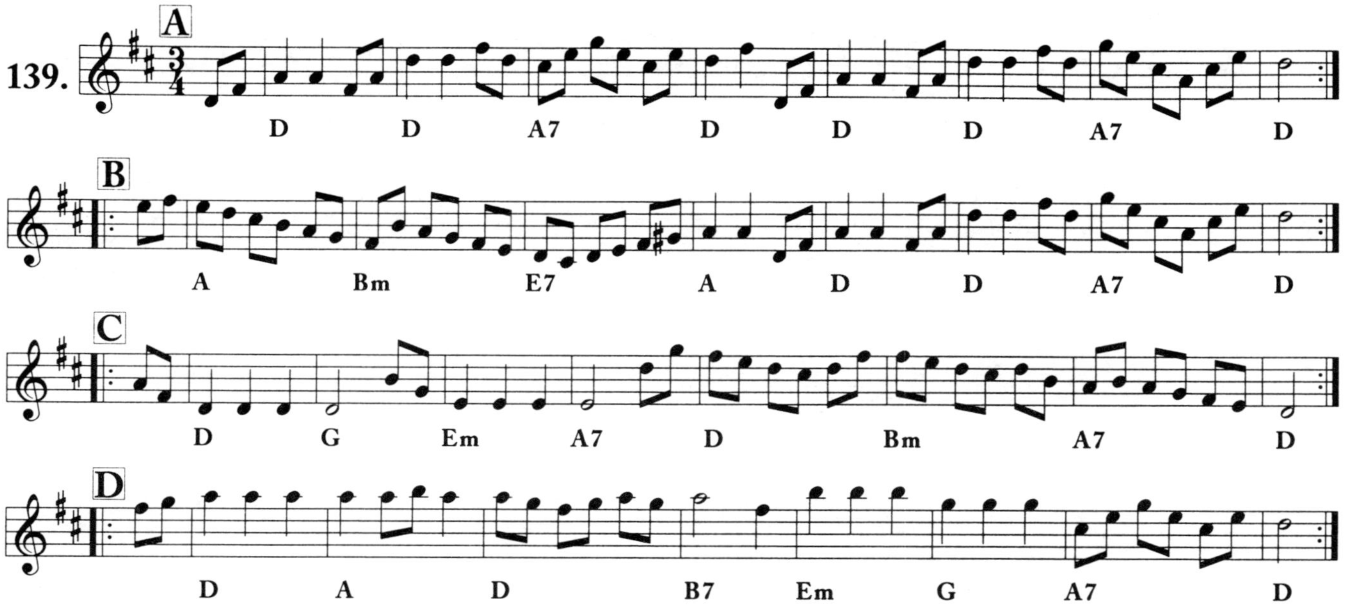

LADY JANE'S

LADY WELLINGTON'S NO. 1

Lady Wellington's No. 2

The Liberty

The Lighthouse

The London

Lord Paget's

Lord Wellington's

MAZURKA No. 1

MAZURKA No. 2

MAZURKA No. 3

MAZURKA No. 4

THE MIDNIGHT

149.

THE MILLTOWN

150.

THE NEXT STOP

151.

The Nottingham

Oliver's

The Orange Bower

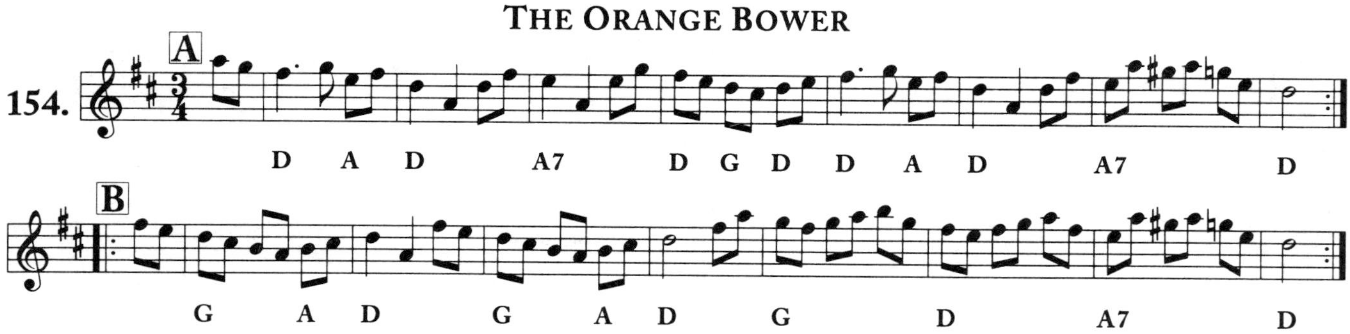

The Overland

THE POLISH

POLLY'S

THE PORTUGESE FANDANGO

THE PRESTON

THE PRINCE'S

(Schwartzenburg's)

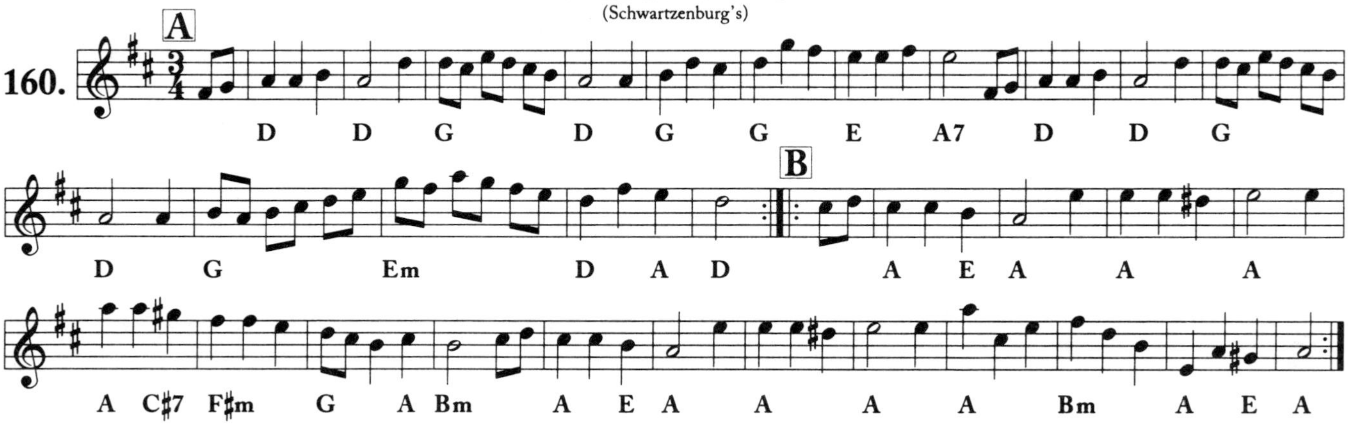

THE PRINCESS OF WALES'

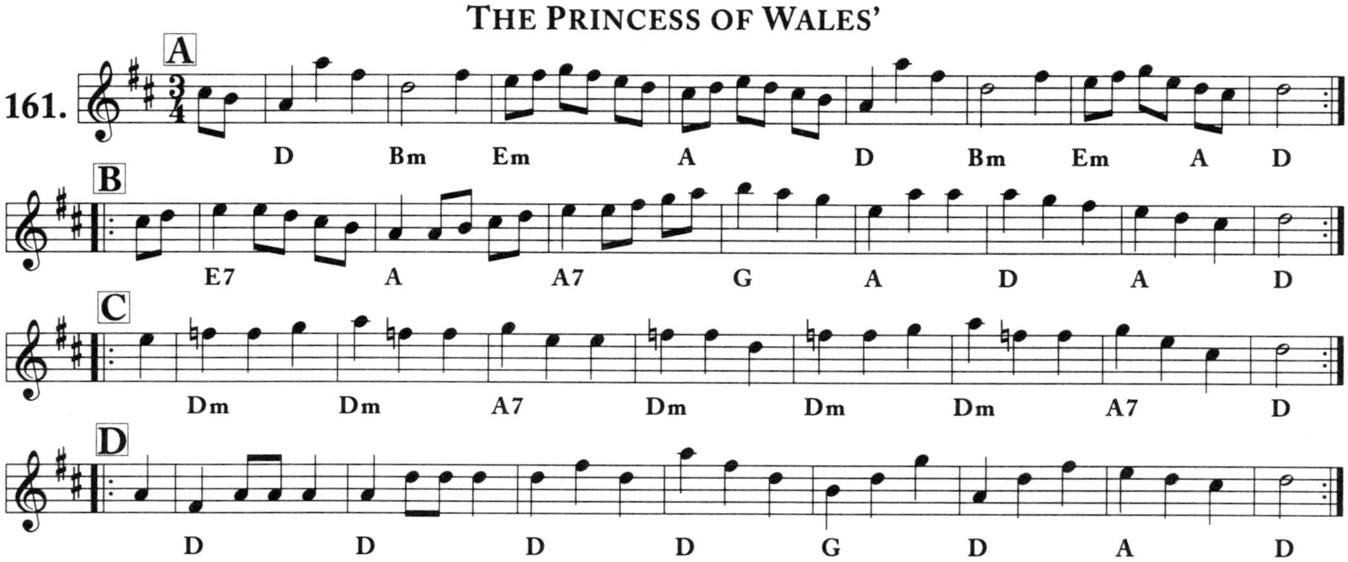

THE QUARRY

THE QUEEN OF PRUSSIA

THE QUEEN OF PRUSSIA'S GRAND

THE QUEEN'S

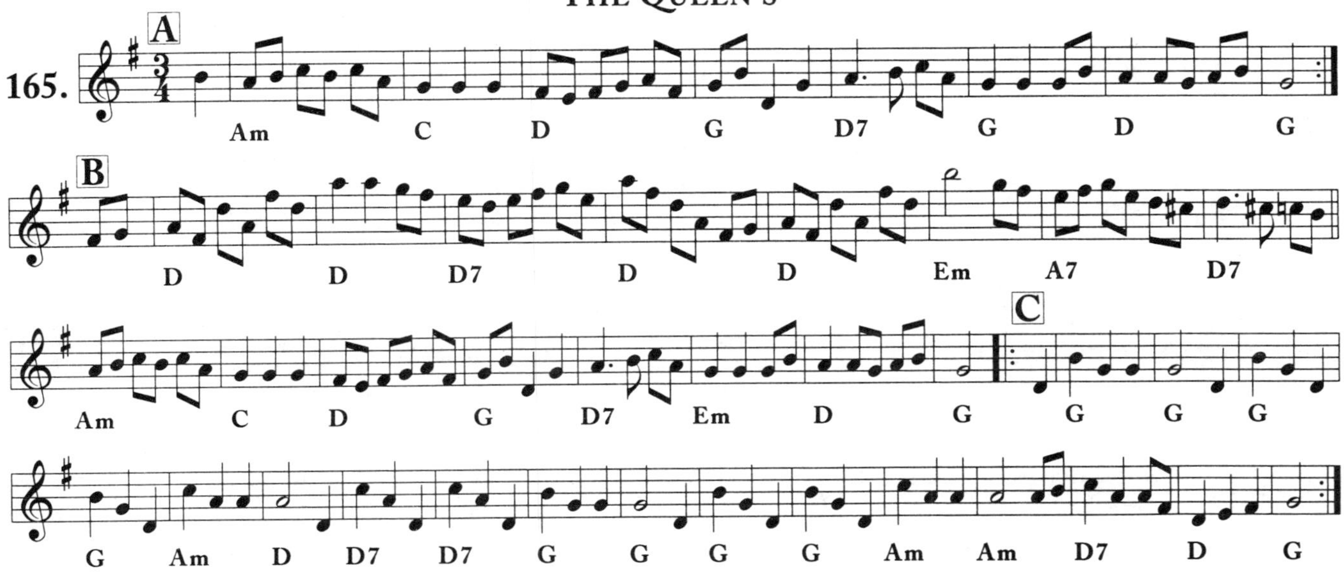

Rackham's

Rags and Stitches

The Revelation

Riondina

THE RUSSIAN

SACKETT'S

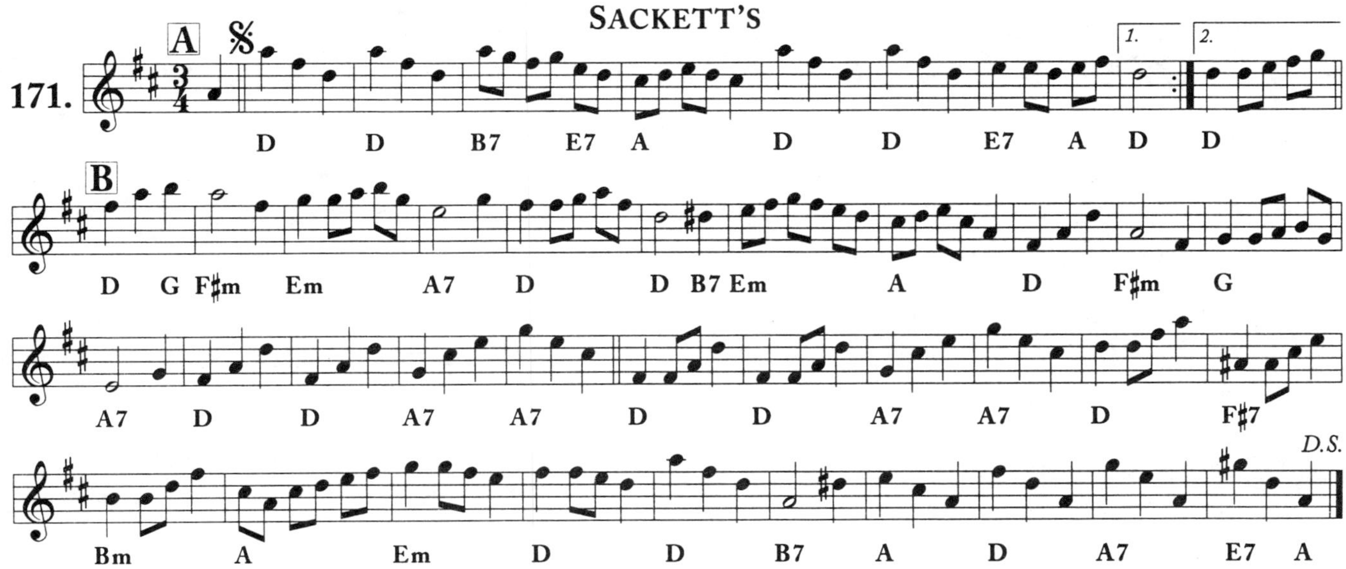

SADLER'S ASCENT

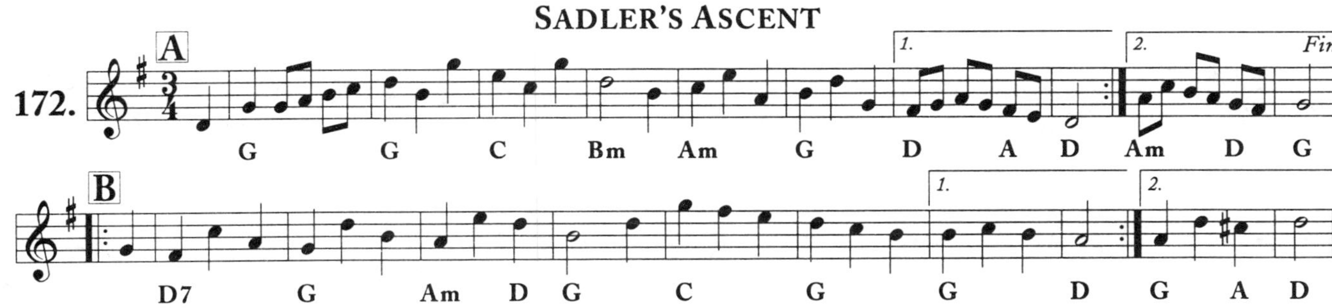

THE SHILLELAGH

THE SICILIAN NO. 1

THE SICILIAN NO. 2

175.

THE SILESIAN

176.

THE SPANISH FANDANGO

177.

The Spanish No. 1

The Spanish No. 2

The Spanish No. 3

The Spanish No. 4

THE STOP

THE SWEDISH

THE SWISS

THE TEATIME

TULLAGH'S

183.

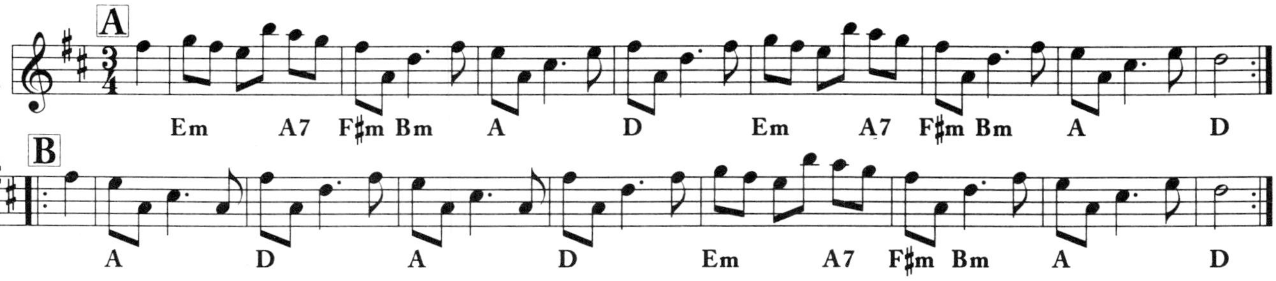

THE TYROLESE

184.

THE UNION

185.

THE USURPER

186.

VARSOVIANA

(Put Your Little Foot)

187.

THE VAUXHALL

188.

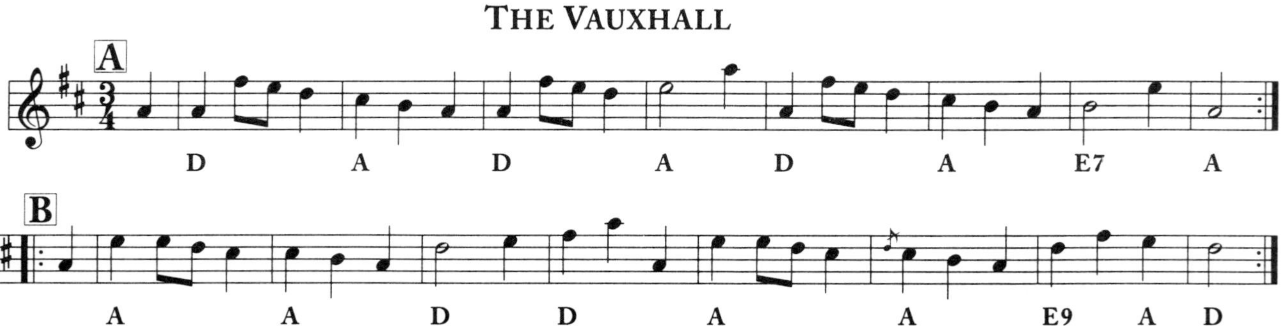

The Victoria

(The Exhibition; The Speaking)

189.

The Virginia

190.

THE VOLUNTEERS'

WATERHOUSE'S

THE WATERLOO

WELLINGTON'S

THE WELSH

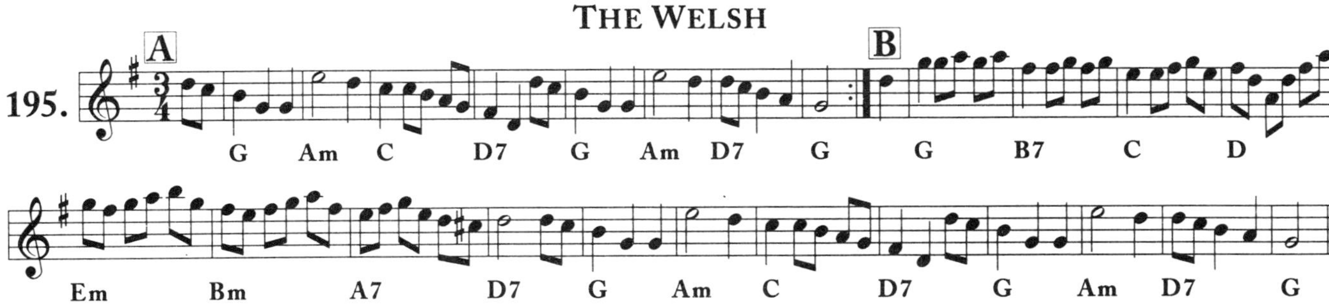

THE WEST WIND

WHITE WINGS

197.

THE WICKLOW

198.

THE YOUGHAL

199.

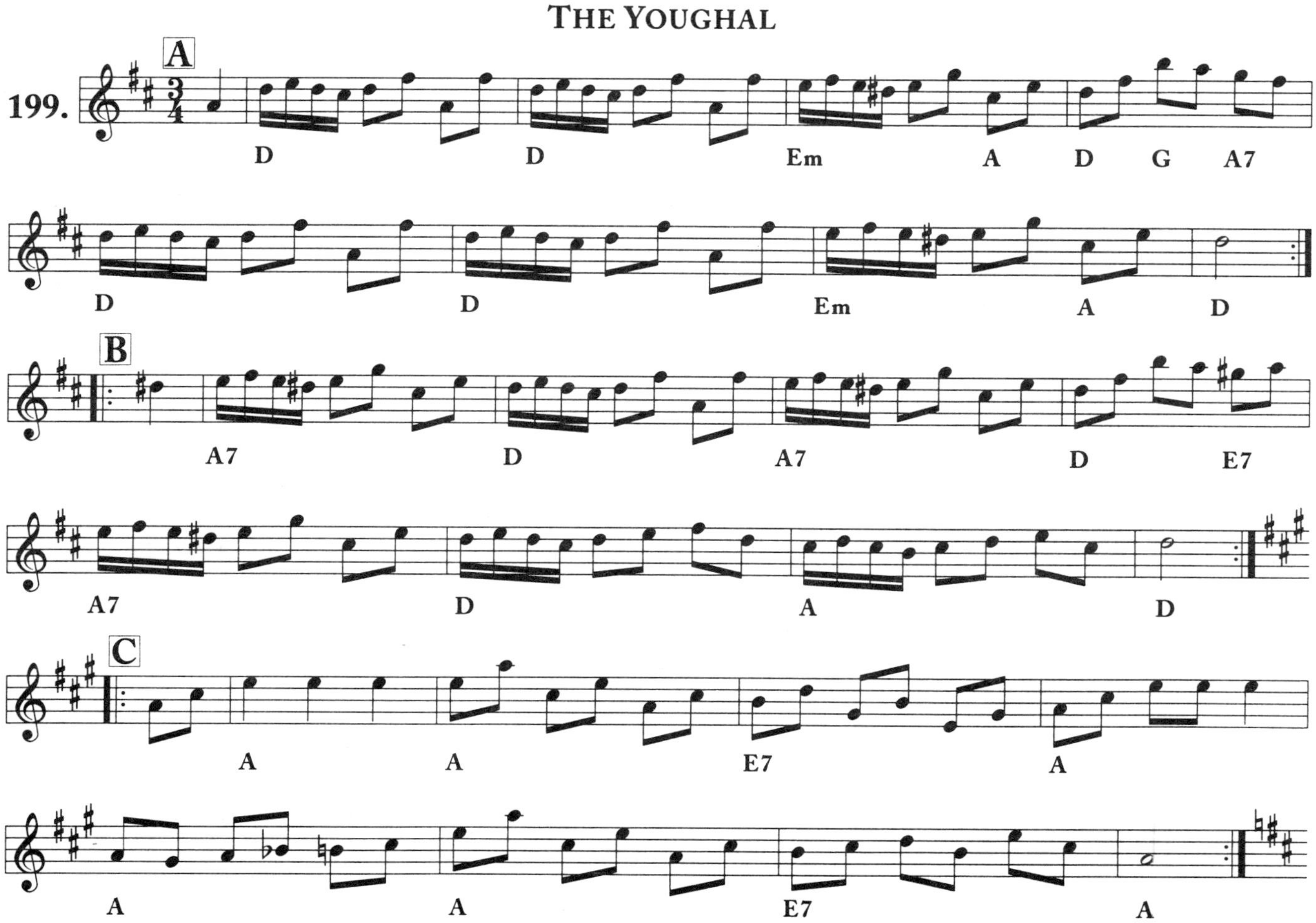

ZEPHYR BREEZES

ALPHABETICAL INDEX TO $\frac{9}{8}$ TUNES

Alternative titles are shown in *italics*

ALPHABETICAL INDEX TO $\frac{9}{8}$ TUNES *continued*

Alternative titles are shown in *italics*

ALPHABETICAL INDEX TO $\frac{3}{4}$ TUNES

Alternative titles are shown in *italics*